Are Muslim Women OPPRESSED?

Beyond the Veil

Zohra Sarwari

Copyright © 2009 by Zohra Sarwari

All rights reserved
Eman Publishing.

Eman Publishing
P.O. Box 404
FISHERS, IN 46038

www.emanpublishing.com

Order Online: www.zohrasarwari.com

All rights reserved. No part of this publication may be reproduced, stored in a retrieval system or transmitted in any form or by any means electronic, mechanical, photocopying, recording or otherwise without the written prior permission of the author.

ISBN 13: 978-0-9823125-1-3
ISBN 10: 0-9823125-1-2
LCCN: 2009901039

EMAN
publishing

Cover Design by Zeeshan Shaikh

Printed in the United States of America

Are Muslim Women OPPRESSED?

Beyond the Veil

Zohra Sarwari

Dedication

'(Our Lord! Accept this from us. You are All-Hearing, the All-Knowing).'

(The Qur'aan: Chapter 2, Verse 127)

Acknowledgment

In the name of Allaah (SWT), the Most Gracious, the Most Magnificent. All praise is due to Allaah (SWT), Lord of the universe. We praise Him, seek His help and His forgiveness, and we seek His protection from the accursed Satan. Whomever Allaah (SWT) guides will never be misguided, and whomever He allows to be misguided will never be guided. I bear witness that there is no deity worthy of worship except Allaah (SWT), who is One; alone and has no partners. I bear witness that Muhammad (PBUH) is His servant and messenger. May the blessings of Allaah (SWT) be upon him, his family, his companions and the righteous that follow them until the Day of Judgment.

I would like to thank my family and friends for all of their support, especially Zeeshan, Madeeha, and Saqib Sheikh, who are an asset to my team masha'Allaah. A very special thanks goes to Dr. Daoud Nassimi for all of his efforts and hard work in editing this book - jazaakAllaahu khayran! May Allaah (SWT) reward you all - ameen!

Terminology

1. "**ALLAAH**" is the Arabic name for THE ONE SUPREME UNIVERSAL GOD.
2. "**SWT**" is an abbreviation of the Arabic words *"Subhaanahu wa Ta'aalaa"* that mean " He is exalted above weakness and indignity."
3. **Qur'aan:** The Book of Allaah. A divine guidance for mankind. The FINAL TESTAMENT.
4. **Muslim** is one who has submitted to the Will of ALLAAH
5. **Hajj** is one of the five pillars of Islam, a duty one must perform during one's life-time if one has the financial resources for it. It must be performed during certain specified dates of Dhul-Hijjah (the twelfth month in the Islamic calendar).
6. **PBUH** means Peace be upon him.
7. **PBUT** means Peace be upon them.
8. **Hijaab** refers to a woman's dress code.
9. **(RA)** stands for *Radiya 'Llaahu 'anhu,* which means "May Allaah be pleased with him."
10. **Insha'Allaah** means God Willing.

Table of Contents

Chapter 1:
Status Of Women In Islam   12

Chapter 2:
Muslim Woman's Attire   20

Chapter 3:
The Position Of A Muslim Daughter   28

Chapter 4:
The Position Of A Muslim Wife   34

Chapter 5:
The Position Of A Muslim Mother   44

Chapter 6:
The Role Of A Muslim Woman In Her Community   54

Chapter 7:
The Role Of A Muslim Woman Being Herself   61

Chapter 1

Status Of Women In Islam

'Often people attempt to live their lives backwards: they try to have more things, or more money, in order to do more of what they want so they will be happier. The way it actually works is the reverse. You must first be who you really are, then, do what you need to do, in order to have what you want.'

Margaret Young

Women are recognized in Islam as full and equal partners of man in the procreation of humans; she becomes the mother, and he becomes the father, and both parents are needed for life. By this partnership, she is entitled to equal rights, as she also undertakes equal responsibilities; her role is not less vital than his role. Both are important and necessary.

     A woman is equal to a man in that she too has responsibilities, and she also receives rewards for the good that she does. A woman is acknowledged as an independent personality. She has aspirations, hopes and dreams, as a man does. She is equal to a man in the desire and need to acquire knowledge and education. She is neither inferior nor deviant in her nature to that of a man's; each of them is a part of one another.

Allaah (SWT) says in the **Qur'aan: Chapter 3, Verse 195:**

> 'And their Lord has accepted (their prayers) and answered them (saying): 'Never will I allow to be lost the work of any of you, be he male or female; you are members, one of another.'

The Prophet, Muhammad (PBUH) said:

> "Seeking knowledge is a duty on every Muslim."

(Reported by Ibn Majah)

History shows us over and over that women went to battles with the men; they were there to nurse them, prepare the supplies, and serve as warriors. They were not considered worthless creatures, shut inside the house, and deprived of rights.

A woman is entitled to freedom of expression as much as a man is. She is entitled to speak out and express herself, and argue and participate in serious talks. This took place during the time of the

Prophet, Muhammad (PBUH), and is noted in the **Qur'aan (Chapter 58, Verses number 1-4)**, as well as during the rule of the Caliph Umar Ibn al-Khattab (RA).

Islam allows women an equal right to enterprise, to earn and possess independently. She has a right to have property, she has a right to live with honor, and her life is as sacred as any man. However, so is her penalty, should she commit a crime. Yet if she is wronged or harmed, she gets due compensation equal to what a man in her position would get. What is profound is that even in the West, in today's society, women don't get the same salary as men in the same position. Women still get underpaid. However, Islam gave women rights over 1400 years ago. Islam gave them rights to own property, to be respected as an individual; not a man's property, to run a business, or work, etc.

The pagan Arabs used to look at women as an inferior entity, and they would feel embarrassed at the birth of a daughter. However, Allaah (SWT) condemns this attitude in the following verse:

> *"And when the news of (the birth of) a female (child) is brought to any of them, his face becomes dark, and he is filled with inward grief! He*

> *hides himself from the people because of the evil of that whereof he has been informed. Shall he keep her with dishonor or bury her in the earth? Certainly, evil is their decision."*

(The Qur'aan: Chapter 16, Verses 58-59)

This is how the pagan Arabs used to act when a female was born to them, and Allaah (SWT) addresses them. Having a daughter, even in this day and age, for many people around the world causes grief. Many people still believe that a son has a higher status. Again this is a result of cultural beliefs and is not a reflection on Islam, for in the eyes of Allaah (SWT) we are all created equal. Allaah (SWT) says in the Qur'aan:

> *"To Allâh belongs the kingdom of the heavens and the earth. He creates what He wills. He bestows female (offspring) upon whom He wills, and bestows male (offspring) upon whom He wills. Or He bestows both males and females, and He renders barren whom He wills.*

*Verily, He is the All-Knower and is
Able to do all things."*

(The Qur'aan: Chapter 16, Verses 49-50)

This is to show us that we have no control over the gender of our children, and we don't know if we will even have any children. We have to be grateful for what we get, and always accept it as a gift, and not a burden.

Islam gave women, 1400 years ago the right to own property. Before Islam, she was not given that right to inherit. Even in America, women didn't have the right to inherit until the last 88 years; it was not until 1920 and the 19th Amendment that women won their natural, human rights of equality.

The great thing about Islamic Law is that regardless of what happens in a family, regardless of the will one writes your right is your right to inherit. The share one receives is based on the justice and fairness of Allaah (SWT). The share designated to a woman is hers; no one can refuse her of it, even if the decease wishes to give it to someone else. In the West when parents fall out with their children they write them off from their wealth; you hear of cases where all the wealth has been left to a pet of the family. Islam protects the individual from such injustice, and ensures that the blood ties are preserved and everyone gets his/her due insha'Allaah. This is done to protect the rights of the heirs.

At certain times, men do receive two shares of inheritance while the female receives only one share; this is because in Islam the man has the sole responsibility of taking care of his wife, family, and any other relatives who may be needy. All financial burdens are on the man and on him alone.

The woman on the other hand has very little financial responsibility, except for her own luxurious expenses. In the case where the woman has no relations on whom she can depend on, then obviously she can't inherit, and there is no one to give her anything. This is when society steps in, and takes care of her; she may be given aid, and if she works, the money that she makes will be hers. In the worst case scenario she is not responsible for anyone else except herself, whereas a man is always responsible for his family, and any of his relations who need help.

Another distinction women have that men don't have is that she is exempt from some religious duties; prayers and fasting during menstruation.

Chapter 2

Muslim Woman's Attire

'A woman's beauty is in whom she is and her actions, not what she looks like or what she wears.'

Zohra Sarwari

This is always a sensitive topic! People are always scared to ask me why Muslim women dress as they do. Often when I am speaking somewhere, I can feel people wanting to ask this question, but they don't. I feel that I need to address this question, to help curb the curiosity of many people out there who are reluctant to ask this question.

Muslim women have been told to observe *hijaab* by the Creator of the world; Allaah (SWT). They only observe *hijaab* when they are outside, or where there are other men who are not immediate family who can see them. In the Qur'aan it says:

> *"Oh Prophet, tell your wives and your daughters and the women of the believers to draw their outer garments close around them. **That will be better, that they may be known (as Muslims) and not be bothered**."*

(The Qur'aan: Chapter 33, Verse 59)

The first and foremost reason one wears the *'hijaab'* is to please Allaah (SWT). However, the *hijaab* is more than just obedience; it is a blessing for a Muslim woman; it is her identity. It is how she acts, thinks, and reacts to the situations around her. Lastly, it is *hijaab* that brings her modesty; people treat her with respect for who she is, and not what she looks like. When a Muslim woman wears the *hijaab* she wants to be identified for her personality, for her intelligence, and not her looks and body. For many women it is one of the biggest hurdles they have to overcome.

People ask, does she have self-esteem; *"I mean is she confident in whom she is? Or does she wear it to hide her faults?"* I always laugh at this one, for if she didn't have confidence and self-esteem, she wouldn't wear it. It is part of her dignity and self-esteem that she doesn't care about what people say, and just wants to obey the commandment of her Lord.

"The hijaab is actually liberating, it frees you from the chains of this world where everyone is so vain and engrossed with the superficial things: such as appearance, clothing, jewelry, etc." says Farzana.

Let's look at the word *hijaab*; *hijaab* comes from the Arabic word *hijaaba*: which means to conceal or hide. The next question might be, to what extent is the covering Allaah (SWT) says in the Qur'aan:

> "Say to the believing men that they should lower their gaze and guard their modesty; that is purer for them. Verily, Allaah is well acquainted with all that they do. And say to the believing women that they should lower their gaze and guard their modesty; and that they should not display their beauty and ornaments except what must ordinarily appear thereof; that they should draw their veils over their bosoms and not display their beauty except to their husbands."

(The Qur'aan: Chapter 24, Verses 30-31)

The two lessons from this for women are:

1. The head covering should be drawn as to cover the hair, the neck, and the bosom.
2. A woman should not show her beauty except what appears naturally.

Islam has no fixed standards as to the style of dress or type of clothing that Muslims must wear. However, in the Qur'aan we are told exactly what needs to be covered and the Prophet, Muhammad (PBUH), who is the final messenger sent to mankind, has also explained the dress code to us:

'Ayesha (R) reported that Asmaa the daughter of Abu Bakr (R) came to the Messenger of Allaah (PBUH) while wearing thin clothing. He approached her and said:

"O Asmaa! When a girl reaches the menstrual age, it is not proper that anything should remain exposed except this and this. He pointed to the face and hands."

(Abu Dawood)

Description of clothing:

- The clothing must be long, and loose; it should not in any way describe the shape of the woman's body.
- The clothing must not be see-through; it defeats the purpose of

concealing it, if you can see through the attire.
- The clothing should not be flashy, and attractive; where it grabs the attention of men or other women.
- She is allowed to wear perfume, but it must not be smelt by men that are not her immediate family. Deodorant is fine, but perfume could attract other men to her scent. Women must not dress to look like men, and men shouldn't dress to look like women.

You may have noticed that some women also cover up their face; they only show their eyes. These women dress this way because the Prophet, Muhammad's (PBUH) wives dressed this way. Some scholars think it is mandatory whilst others do not deem it necessary, although it is highly recommended.

The *hijaab* of a Muslim woman doesn't only mean being covered on the outside. It also entails her speech, behavior, manners, and appearance in public; her attire is only one part of it.

Muslim men also have requirements of *'hijaab'*; they are to be covered from the naval to the knee, and are not allowed to wear gold or silk. I would like to refer you to the verse of the Qur'aan that was previously cited; note that it mentions men first and then women!

> *"Say to the believing men that they should lower their gaze and guard their modesty; that is purer for them. Verily, Allaah is well acquainted with all that they do. And say to the believing women that they should lower their gaze and guard their modesty; and that they should not display their beauty and ornaments except what must ordinarily appear thereof; that they should draw their veils over their bosoms and not display their beauty except to their husbands."*
>
> ***(The Qur'aan: Chapter 24, Verses 30-31)***

Chapter 3

The Position Of A Muslim Daughter

'A daughter is as precious as a jewel, as loving as can be, and priceless for all to see.'

Zohra Sarwari

What is the role of a Muslim daughter? First I will address what the role of a daughter to Arabs was prior to Islam, and then how Islam changed that. In the Arab world prior to Islam, fathers would think of their daughters as a bad omen; they would think she couldn't defend their families, like a man could; she couldn't take care of her parents as she would get married and take care of her own family. This belief basically meant that daughters were useless, and this allowed the fathers to bury them alive for fear of poverty, or fear of disgrace which she might bring upon the family when she grew up. This was during the time of pagan worship. Some laws even allowed the father the right to sell his daughter if he wished to do that, and yet other laws allowed him to give his daughter to another man to own or kill, if the former killed the other man's daughter. What an unfortunate state to be in if you were a female at that time. That is oppression.

The Qur'aan states:

"And when the female (infant) buried alive (as the pagan Arabs used to do) shall be questioned. For what sin was she killed?"

(The Qur'aan: Chapter 81, Verses 8-9)

The Qur'aan also states the reactions of the fathers when daughters are born to them:

"And when the news of (the birth of) a female (child) is brought to any of them, his face becomes dark, and he is filled with inward grief! He hides himself from the people because of the evil of that whereof he has been informed. Shall he keep her with dishonor or bury her in the earth? Certainly, evil is their decision."

(The Qur'aan: Chapter 16, Verses 58-59)

What is amazing is that in Islam the girl is actually just as special as the boy. They are both a gift from Allaah (SWT):

"He bestows female (offspring) upon whom He wills, and bestows male (offspring) upon whom He wills. Or He bestows both male and females, and He renders barren whom He

wills. Verily, He is the All-Knower and is Able to do all things."

(The Qur'aan: Chapter 42, Verses 49 – 50)

The Prophet, Muhammad (PBUH) said:

"A Muslim who has two daughters whom he treats well when they accompany him or when he accompanies them, is admitted to Paradise."

(Bukhari)

This shows us that someone who has daughters and treats them well will have a place in paradise; thus treating a female well is that important! The birth of a girl was no longer a burden but a great blessing!

The Prophet Muhammad (PBUH) led by example; how his daughter had a great place in his heart.

"Fatima is part of me; what makes her angry makes me angry."

(Bukhari)

As for the daughter's rights upon the father, he has to pay for her education as he does for her brothers. Her upkeep is obligatory on him until she marries. If she doesn't marry it will be until her father is alive. Her father does not have the right to sell her, or make her the property of another person.

In addition, the father does not have the right to marry his daughter to a man she hates and does not approve of. He must ask her opinion of the man she is going to marry. If the daughter says no, then he has no power to force her into that marriage. If the father or the person in charge marries the widow, divorcee, or single girl to a man without her permission, the contract is invalid and revocable.

Islamic Law also commands that the mother also be consulted in the marriage of her daughter, this way the marriage can be to the satisfaction of everyone.

The daughter, like the son, also has to be obedient to her parents; she should listen to them and respect them.

Chapter 4

The Position Of A Muslim Wife

'A wife is the foundation of how high the building will be.'

Zohra Sarwari

History indicates that in the old days women were seen to be impure, and created by Satan. What this meant was that men would be more pure and pious if they lived in solitaire and worshiped God. Others considered women to be a slave for men; she was the one who cooked, served, and did what the husband pleased.

Islam came to erase all that; a man was to marry and not live a monastic life. Islam established that you could marry and still be a devout man or woman. As a matter of fact Islam urges marriage, and tells us that marriage is a great thing:

"And among His signs is this, that He created for you wives from among yourselves, that you may find repose in them, and He has put between you affection and mercy. Verily, in that are indeed signs for a people who reflect."

(The Qur'aan: Chapter 30, Verse 21)

During the time of the Prophet, Muhammad (PBUH), three companions just wanted to devote their entire lives to worshipping Allaah (SWT). One wanted to fast all day, another wanted to spend the whole night in worship, and the third one was not going to get married. The Prophet, Muhammad (PBUH) said:

"Are you the people who said such a thing? By Allaah I am the most fearing of God among you, the most pious, but I fast and then break my fast, I wake up at night to worship Allaah and I sleep, and I marry. Whoever does not follow my way (Sunnah), he is not one of us."

(Bukhari)

This shows us that the Prophet (PBUH) said that everything should be done in moderation; extremism in any form is wrong.

Islam has also raised the status of women by identifying the fact that a good wife is the key to happiness, after belief in Allaah and following His commands.

The Prophet, Muhammad (PBUH) told Umar:

> *"Shall I tell you the best a man can treasure? It is a good wife. If he looks at her, she gives him pleasure; if he orders her, she obeys; and if he is away from her, she remains faithful to him."*

(Abu Dawud)

The Prophet Muhammad (PBUH) said:

> *"The world is delightful and its greatest treasure is a good woman."*

(Muslim)

He (PBUH) also said:

> *"Whoever is granted a good wife, he is helped to follow half his religion, let him obey God in the second half."*

(Al-Targheeb wal-Tarheeb)

He (PBUH) also said:

> *"There are three things that cause happiness and three things that create misery for the human being. A good wife, a good house, and good transport cause*

happiness. A bad woman, a bad house and bad transport cause his misery."

(Ahmad)

Islam has given the married woman rights: the first right is a dowry. If a Muslim man wants to marry her, he has to give her a dowry, as a symbol of his desire in wanting to marry her:

"And give to the women (whom you marry) their Mahr (obligatory bridal gift given by the husband to his wife at the time of marriage) with a good heart, but if they, of their own good pleasure remit a part of it to you, take it, and enjoy it without fear of any harm (as Allaah has made it lawful)."

(The Qur'aan: Chapter 4, Verse 4)

The words *"with a good heart"* mean that this is a gift from the man to the woman. A lot of people make the mistake of thinking it is a price for her giving him pleasure. Look around other civilizations, where it is a woman who has to pay for the marriage and other things, though by nature it is a man who requests more from her. She is the one who does the cooking, the cleaning, she bears the children, raises them etc. Islam recognizes the value of a woman.

She also has the right to maintenance: the husband is required to provide food, shelter, clothing, a place to live, and costs of medical treatment, according to his environment, conditions and income:

> *"Let the rich man spend according to his means, and the man whose resources are restricted, let him spend according to what Allaah has given him. Allaah puts no burden on any person beyond what He has given him."*

(The Qur'aan: Chapter 65, Verse 7)

The Prophet, Muhammad (PBUH) said:

> *"A believer must not hate his wife, and if he is displeased with one bad quality in her, then let him be pleased with one that is good in her."*

(Muslim)

She also has the right to live with him in peace:

"And live with them honorably."

(The Qur'aan: Chapter 4, Verse 19)

The Prophet Muhammad (PBUH) said:

"The best of you is he who is the best to his family, and I am the best to my family."

(Transmitted by Ibn Hibban Charity (El-Ehsan))

As for the wife, she is obliged to obey her husband in everything except disobeying Allaah (SWT); she is to take care of his money, not to spend it without his permission. As for his home, she is not to allow anyone in his home, except with his permission, even if it is a relative. Islam is a fair religion; it is fair towards both the husband and the wife:

"And they (women) have rights (over their husbands as regards living expenses, etc.) similar (to those of their husbands) over them (as regards obedience and respect, etc.) to what is reasonable."

(The Qur'aan: Chapter 2, Verse 228)

In Islam a married woman does not have to give up her last name; the woman is her own self, and she has her own personality. She can still make contracts by herself; she can buy and sell. She can give her own money away in charity, to her family, or just keep it herself. In the West these rights have only recently been given to married women and in other countries some women even today are restricted by their husbands. The Qur'aan discusses marriage, consultation and divorce:

"Should they (husband and wife) wish to separate from each other in agreement and upon consultation then they can do so blamelessly."

(The Qur'aan: Chapter 2, Verse 232)

Similarly, with reference to divorce:

"And it is not lawful for you (men) to take back (from your wives) any of your gifts which you have given them, except when both parties fear that they would be unable to keep the limits ordained by Allaah (e.g. to deal with each other on a fair basis). Then if you fear that they would not be able to keep the limits ordained by Allaah, then

there is no sin on either of them if she gives something for her freedom."

(The Qur'aan: Chapter 2, Verse 229)

"And live with them (wives) in kindness. For if you dislike them - perhaps you dislike a thing and Allaah brings therein much good."

(The Qur'aan: Chapter 4, Verse 19)

You can see from all the above that the role of a Muslim woman as a wife is a noble role, and one that is respected highly; she is not an object, but someone who is respected and loved.

Chapter

5

The Position Of A Muslim Mother

'It is a Muslim mother's strength, knowledge, patience and wisdom that raise the children to be who they become.'

Zohra Sarwari

'And We have enjoined upon man [care] for his parents. His mother carried him, [increasing her] in weakness upon weakness, and his weaning is in two years. Be grateful to Me and to your parents; to Me is the [final] destination. But if they endeavor to make you associate with Me that of which you have no knowledge, do not obey them but accompany them in [this] world with appropriate kindness and follow the way of those who turn back to Me [in repentance]. Then to Me will be your return, and I will inform you about what you used to do.'

(The Qur'aan: Chapter 31, Verse14-15)

'And We have enjoined upon man goodness to parents. But if they endeavor to make you associate with Me that of which you have no knowledge, do not obey

them. To Me is your return and I will inform you about what you used to do.'

(The Qur'aan: Chapter 29, Verse 8)

The above two verses show that Allaah (SWT) wants a Muslim to respect his/her parents. He wants him/her to be grateful to them and have the most beautiful conduct towards them. Allaah (SWT) also shows us what the mother goes through; bearing the child, and then delivering the child, and then weaning the child for 2 years. He shows us the hardships moms face. Only when one's parents order him/her to disobey Allaah and His Prophet, Muhammad (PBUH) is when the child should not obey his/her parents, but even then the child must have good conduct and relations with his/her parents.

Being grateful and thanking the Lord of the world is common sense, yet I know many who don't do it. We cannot say 'thank you' enough for all those things that we take for granted, such as our eyesight, hearing, speaking abilities, etc. Even if we were to count all the blessings Allaah (SWT) has bestowed upon us we couldn't, just the basic necessities that we are born with are countless.

Now let's look at how many people actually thank their parents for all that they have gone through for them. All you hear in this day and age is people complaining about their parents. God the Greatest has commanded us to give thanks to our parents, obey them, and respect them:

> *'And your Lord has decreed that you worship none but Him. And that you be dutiful to your parents. If one of them or both of them attain old age in your life, say not to them a word of disrespect, nor shout at them but address them in terms of honor. And lower unto them the wing of submission and humility through mercy, and say: "My Lord! Bestow on them Your Mercy as they did bring me up when I was young."'*

(The Qur'aan: Chapter 17, Verse 23-24)

This is a profound verse, for Allaah (SWT) is asking us to be patient and dutiful to our parents as they attain old age. So much so that we don't even say the word *"uff"* (This is an expression of the least level of discomfort). We are to address them with honor and respect and pray for them. Parents; no matter how difficult they can be, we have to be patient and remember all of the things they did for us, and Allaah (SWT) keeps reminding us about the importance of this.

What is so sad to see is that more and more people put their parents in nursing homes while they can support them; they don't care about them. I have experienced this firsthand when I worked in a nursing home. I was devastated to see that not only did people put their parents there, but they also didn't go to visit them; it's as if they don't exist, and their worldly lives are more important than their old aged parents. I tell myself this first, and then speak to you as my readers, take care of your parents.

Next, I will discuss what the Prophet Muhammad (PBUH) said on the subject of 'mothers':

The Prophet (PBUH) said:

"Paradise is under the feet of mothers."

(Ahmad)

'The Messenger of Allaah, may Allaah bless him and grant him peace, said, *"Shall I tell you which is the worst of the major wrong actions?"*

They replied, *"Yes, Messenger of Allaah."*

He said, *"Associating something else with Allaah and disobeying parents."* He had been reclining, but then he sat up and said,

"And false witness."'

(Bukhari)

'Jahmah narrated: I said to the Prophet, *"O Messenger of Allaah, I desire to go on a (military) expedition and I have come to consult you."*

He asked me if I had a mother and when I replied that I had, he said, *"Stay with her because Paradise lies beneath her feet."'*

(Ahmad)

'I asked the Prophet, Muhammad (PBUH) who has the greatest right over a man, and he said, *"His mother."'*

'I asked, *"Messenger of Allaah, who is most worthy of my company?"*

He replied, *"Your mother."*

I asked, *"Then whom?"* He replied, *"Your mother."*

I asked, *"Then whom?"* He replied, *"Your mother."*

I asked, *"Who is most worthy of my company?"*

He replied, *"Your father, and then the next closest relative and then the next."'*

(Bukhari & Muslim)

"Your Lord has decreed that you worship none save Him, and that you be kind to your parents."

(The Qur'aan: Chapter 17, Verse 23)

The Prophet (PBUH) said:

'When I stand for prayer, I intend to prolong it but on hearing the cries of a child, I cut it short, as I dislike troubling the child's mother.'

(Bukhari)

The Prophet (PBUH) said,

> *"Allaah has forbidden for you (1) **to be undutiful to your mothers**, (2) to bury your daughters alive, (3) to not to pay the rights of others (e.g. charity etc.) and (4) to beg of men (begging). And Allaah has hated for you (1) vain, useless talk, or that you talk too much about others, (2) to ask too many questions, (in disputed religious matters) and (3) to waste the wealth (by extravagance)."*

(Bukhari)

Narrated by Aishah:

> *'A poor woman came to me with her daughters. I gave her three date-fruits. She gave a date to each of them and then she took up one date-fruit and brought that to her mouth to eat, but her daughters asked her for that also. She then divided between them the date fruit that she intended to eat. This (kind) treatment of her impressed me and I mentioned that to Allaah's Messenger (PBUH) who said, "Verily Allah has assured Paradise*

> *for her, because of (this act) of hers,"* or said, *"HE (glory be to Him) has rescued her from Hell-Fire."'*

> **(Bukhari)**

The status of a woman in Islam as a mother is a noble status. To be a mother is a blessing, as it is to be a father. The status of motherhood isn't a low status, one that people regret, but rather it is a blessing from Allaah (SWT) as being a mother and fulfilling her responsibilities may lead her to the gates of paradise. Unfortunately, in the time we live in, women don't want to be mothers. They see it as a burden. Many people feel confined by having children. They want children because it seems like a good idea, but when the child cries or whines, or yells, the parent wants to give up the duty.

I am here to say, that being a mom is a blessing and not a burden. Islam has taught me this more than anything else; yes I have hard days like all moms do, but it only encourages me to try harder for the sake of Allaah (SWT). *"Paradise must be won"*, this is the saying that motivates me day in and day out. Nothing in life is worth enjoying without some effort and hard work, and parenting is the same way.

Chapter

6

The Role Of A Muslim Woman In Her Community

'It might take a community to raise one child, but it takes one woman to build a community.'

Zohra Sarwari

As you know women make up half of society. Usually it is the woman who nurtures and takes care of the children, husband and even the elderly. It is the woman who cares about her community, and her neighbors. The woman's role in the community is nothing but magnificent. She is the leader in her home, as well as her community. It is the woman who teaches the faith, values, and morals to the children, men, other women, and society. Of course this is all by the Will of Allaah (SWT).

In many other religions or creeds it states that women are evil or impure, and the followers of those religions believe that God says this.

Prophet, Muhammad (PBUH) said:

"A believer is never impure."

(Bukhari)

Allaah, The Exalted, created Adam from clay and Eve from Adam, and mankind came from both of them:

'O mankind, fear your Lord, who created you from a single soul and created from it its mate and dispersed from both of them many men and women.'

(The Qur'aan: Chapter 4, Verse 1)

'It is He Who created you from a single soul, and made his mate of like nature, in order that he might dwell with her (in love).'

(The Qur'aan: Chapter 7, Verse 189)

The Muslim woman's role in the community starts at home. Her role in the home is a huge job; she has to take care of the family, and prepare the home as a place of comfort. This role is a noble role, and should not be underestimated or neglected.

Often when one asks a woman what she does, and she replies that she is a housewife, other men and women look at her with disgust, as though she is insignificant and her job is the lowest job. Basically, they look at her thinking, *'That's not a real skill, anybody could do that.'*

People don't respect or appreciate what housewives do, thus this attitude has made women in the West feel as if they need to do more to be respected by society, by their spouses, and even by their own children.

I want to explain something to all of you who are reading this book; a woman's job in the house is just as hard if not harder than all of the other careers out there. In fact at some point or another she employs the various skills of various jobs. Her role consists of but is not limited to the list below:

- She has to have the skills to cook (Chef)
- She has to have the skills to teach her kids (Teacher)
- She has to have the skills to practice patience and perseverance.
- She has to have the skills to multi-task (Manager)
- She has to have the skills to bring peace in the family (Negotiator)
- She has to have the skills to think about her neighbors
- She has to have the skills to take care of her parents and her husband's parents (Care Taker)

- She has to have the skills to sew (Seamstress)
- She has to have the skills to shop accordingly (Buyer)
- She has to have the skills to clean effectively (Cleaner)
- She has to have the skills to manage her time accordingly
- She has to make time not to forget herself
- She has to make time to worship
- She has to make time to visit the sick and much more (Nurse)

While to some people this may seem like a career not worth mentioning or a career with little value, I value this woman tremendously. Islam values this woman greatly. This woman is sacrificing herself for her family. This woman is sacrificing her career for her family. When the time is right this woman might work, she might have additional duties, but for now her family comes first. Next time you meet a Muslim woman and you ask her what she does, and she says 'she is a homemaker,' treat her with the same respect you would treat any other woman, regardless of her career.

The next two verses from the Qur'aan give women, as well as men, the right to enjoin good and forbid evil:

"The believing men and the believing women are responsible for each other. They enjoin the good and forbid the evil."

(The Qur'aan: Chapter 9, Verse 71)

"Let there arise out of you a group of people inviting to all that is good and forbidding all evil. And it is they who are the successful."

(The Qur'aan: Chapter 3, Verse 104)

The two verses stated above allow a woman to vote, should she be in a country where voting is permissible; by voting she is able to voice her opinion as to whom she thinks is a better candidate.

Women in the community can also pursue their careers; they could be doctors, lawyers, engineers, teachers, etc. It all depends on what they are educated and trained for.

Chapter 7

The Role Of A Muslim Woman Being Herself

'Never settle for less, be all that you were meant to be, for you are unique.'

Zohra Sarwari

Many allegations have been made by distorted religious teachings that have attributed lies to Allaah (SWT). One of those lies is claiming that it was Eve who seduced Adam into eating from the tree. In the next verse from the Qur'aan you will read what happened between Adam and Eve (PBUT):

"O, Adam dwell you and your wife in the Garden, and eat thereof as you both wish: but approach not this tree, lest you become of the unjust. Then Satan whispered suggestions to them, in order to uncover that which was hidden from them (before); he said: 'Your Lord only forbade you this tree, lest you should become angels or such beings as live for ever.' And he (Satan) swore to them both, (saying) that he was their sincere advisor."

(The Qur'aan: Chapter 7, Verses 19-21)

Then both Adam and Eve (PBUT) repented together:

"They said: 'Our Lord, we have wronged our own souls: If You forgive us not and bestow not upon us Your Mercy, we shall certainly be lost.'"

(The Qur'aan: Chapter 7, Verse 23)

"Then did Satan make them slip from the (Garden), and get them out of the state (of felicity) in which they had been."

(The Qur'aan: Chapter 2, Verse 36)

A woman is just as responsible as a man for her religious duties to Allaah (SWT). Even if her family, including her husband disagrees with her, she is still held accountable for her beliefs, and practicing them correctly.

The Muslim woman like the Muslim man is to believe in Allaah (SWT), His Books, His Angels, The Day of Judgment, His Messengers and the Divine Decree. She too would have to pray her daily prayers, fast in the month of Ramadhaan, pay Zakaah (Obligatory charity), and make the pilgrimage (Hajj) to Makkah (if she has the financial and physical ability to do so).

Allaah (SWT) addresses everyone, men and women, equally, in the Qur'aan:

> *"The Muslim men and the Muslim women, the believing men and the believing women, the worshipping men and the worshipping women, the truthful men and the truthful women, the pious men and the pious women, the alms-giving men and the alms-giving women, the fasting men and the fasting women, the men who are chaste and the women who are chaste, the men who remember Allaah much and the women who do likewise, Allaah has prepared a forgiveness and a great reward for all."*

(The Qur'aan: Chapter 33, Verse 35)

Taking Care of Herself

Cleanliness

The Muslim woman must take care of her appearance as should any Muslim. The Prophet, Muhammad (PBUH) told his Companions, when they were traveling to meet some brothers in faith:

"You are going to visit your brothers, so repair your saddles and make sure that you are dressed well, so that you will stand out among people like an adornment, for Allaah (SWT) does not love ugliness."

(Abu Dawud)

Islam encourages cleanliness so much so that the Prophet, Muhammad (PBUH) said:

"Cleanliness is half of faith."

(Muslim)

Islam taught us about bathing and cleanliness about 1500 years ago. The five times that a Muslim goes and makes ablution, this act alone shows us that a Muslim cleans the places that are most exposed to germs and dirt at least 5 times a day. Back in those days there were no hygienic habits, nor did scientists or researchers discover the effects of cleanliness. It wasn't even discovered around the world 1000 years ago.

Eating Healthy

The Muslim woman like any other woman is encouraged to eat healthy, exercise, and take care of her appearance.

> *"Eat and drink: but waste not by excess, for Allaah loves not the wasters."*
>
> **(The Qur'aan: Chapter 7, Verse 31)**

The Prophet (PBUH) also advised moderation in food and drink:

> *"There is no worse vessel for the son of Adam to fill than his stomach, but if he must fill it, then let him allow one-third for food, one-third for drink, and one-third for air."*
>
> **(Ahmad)**

Exercise

A personal opinion of mine and many others are that a Muslim woman should be exercising 4-5 days a week to keep her body strong and healthy. It's quite funny, because most people think that if a Muslim wears clothes which are baggy, that will help her to hide the fat. I laugh at that one all the time, and say, *"She shouldn't wear it to hide the fat, but to obey her Lord's commandment."*

We all know that when one exercises one's body gets stronger and you develop more stamina and energy and thus get more done. Exercise is also great for helping fight the onset of diseases.

Brushing Teeth

A Muslim woman uses *'miswaak'* to brush her teeth, as well as a toothbrush and toothpaste. Her mouth must smell clean.

"The Messenger of Allaah (PBUH) never woke from sleeping at any time of day or night without cleaning his teeth with a miswaak before performing wudhu."

(Ahmad)

"A'ishah (May Allaah be pleased with her) used to be very diligent in taking care of her teeth: she never

neglected to clean them with a miswaak."

(Bukhari)

The Prophet, Muhammad (PBUH) said:

"Whoever eats onions, garlic or leeks should not approach our mosque, because whatever offends the sons of Adam may offend the angels."

(Muslim)

Hair

The Messenger of Allaah (PBUH) said:

"Whoever has hair let him look after it properly."

(Abu Dawud)

This means that one has to wash their hair, cut it, comb it, and take care of it. A woman who is at home should style her hair for herself, and her husband. She should beautify herself for him, as should the husband for her.

Appearance

A woman must dress in appropriate clothing, and it must be neat and clean. She should make sure her clothes are ironed, and washed. She does not need to go crazy with her looks, and over exaggerate in her clothing or herself; because whilst looking nice and neat is important, too much fashion, and adornment on her will lose the purpose of the *hijaab*; modesty. She should neither exaggerate nor neglect herself. Moderation is the key to the way one should live in Islam.

Intelligence

A Muslim woman is obligated to study and be educated. She should be able to study her religion, as well as other sciences, and life skills. Ignorance breeds ignorance. It is knowledge that opens our eyes, heart and mind to what is truly happening around us. When we let other people choose how and what we should think, we lose who we are. It is knowledge that makes us question our way of life, our purpose in life, and to seek the answers. Most people in the world allow others to dictate to them how to live their lives. This might work for some time, but after a while they lose that battle.

A woman needs not only to pursue her religious studies, but also life skills. The more one knows the more valuable they are to their families and society as a whole. You can never have enough knowledge in your head.

'But say, `O my Lord! Advance me in knowledge.'

(The Qur'aan: Chapter 20, Verse 114)

"Seeking knowledge is a duty on every Muslim."

(Ibn Majah)

If the women are not educated then it becomes difficult to raise intelligent and courageous children. Like the western saying goes, *"Behind every great man is a great woman."* This quote shows us that it is a strong woman that helps her family grow and be the best it can be.

The Prophet Muhammad (PBUH) said:

"Allaah (SWT) loves for any of you, when he does something, to do it well."

(al-Bayhaqi in Shu'ab al-iman)

This means that whatever task we undertake we should put in 100% effort, and do it the best we can *insha'Allaah*- God willing. A great example of this would be the 'Mother of the Believers'- 'A'ishah (May Allaah be pleased with her). She was not only knowledgeable in understanding the matters of religion; she was equally intelligent in history, poetry, medicine, literature, and other branches of knowledge that existed at that time. She was also a charismatic speaker; when she spoke people listened, and were moved by her speech.

"I heard the speeches of Abu Bakr, `Umar, `Uthman, `Ali and the khulafa' who came after them, but I never heard any speech more eloquent and beautiful than that of `A'ishah."

(Tirmidhi)

For the Muslim women, and men she is a great example, and there have been many more since her time. A mind can only grow and develop into something mature, through wisdom and insight of correct, useful and beneficial knowledge.

Worship

A Muslim woman finds time to worship her Lord. During her prayers she finds a quiet place and concentrates and contemplates over the meaning of the Qur'aan. Each prayer is a time for a Muslim to assess him/herself; to correct his/her behavior if they have done or said something wrong.

A true Muslim woman will be able to correct herself, repent, and seek forgiveness from Allaah (SWT) during her prayers, if she has made errors in the day. I guarantee you that as humans we err throughout the day. The prayers are a way to get back on track and try to do the right thing.

Friends

A Muslim woman keeps righteous friends who help her become a better person, who help her develop good character and habits. Our friends are a reflection of us. Remember the old saying "Judge a person by the company they keep."

A Muslim woman is unique and an individual to be respected for who she is.

In conclusion, by now it is clear that the status of women in Islam is exceptionally high and suitable to her nature. Her rights and duties are equal to that of man but not exactly identical with them. If she is withheld of one thing in some aspect, she is fully counterbalanced for it with more things in many other ways. The fact that she is a woman has everything to do with the fact that she should be treated with respect, honor, and without prejudice. Islam does exactly that for the Muslim woman.

Get these other Books that will also inspire and motivate you Insha'Allaah (God Willing)

9 Steps to Achieve Your Destiny
Become the Change that You Envision in this World

9 Steps to Achieve Your Destiny *explores the steps that, if practiced daily, will change your life. God-willing. It shows you how your thinking and habits can make you either successful or stagnant, and helps you navigate your way to right choices and productive habits.*

Imagine That Today is Your Last Day

How would you be if you knew that today was the last day of your life?

Imagine That Today is Your Last Day *reveals to you the secrets of living a great life and accepting your fate when it arrives. The book discusses the missing link in your life for which you will have to pay a price after death. Bring every moment to life, it can be your LAST day TODAY! It is an experience that many never think about, let alone go through it.*

NO! I AM NOT A TERRORIST!

'Terrorism' and 'terrorist' are the latest media buzzwords! However, do you actually know what each of these terms mean? Do you know who a 'terrorist' is? What comes to your mind when you think of a 'terrorist'? Is it a man with a beard, or is it a woman in a veil? Muslims worldwide are being stereotyped and labeled as 'terrorists'. Have you ever stopped and wondered why? Have you ever made the time to discover what lies under the beard and the dress? Have you ever stopped to think what Islam actually has to say about 'terrorism'? Find the answers to all the above questions and more in this book, **'NO! I AM NOT A TERRORIST!'**

Powerful Time Management Skills for Muslims

Islam holds Muslims responsible for every action they do and they will be held answerable for the things they are blessed with and how they used it. One of these blessings is 'Time'. **Powerful Time Management Skills for Muslims** *is explaining using references from the Quran and Sunnah how Muslims should live their lives and utilize the precious gift of 'Time'.*

Speaking Skills Every Muslim Must Know

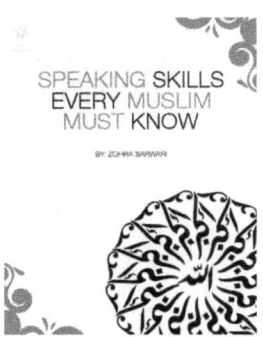

Confidence is the key to success. **Speaking Skills Every Muslim Must Know** *shares with you some vital methods and techniques to develop confidence and helps you overcome your fear of public speaking. The book guides you following the pattern applied by the Prophet Muhammad(PBUH) and how he delivered his speeches.*

Time Management for Success
(E-book)

Become a Professional Speaker Today
(E-book)

Special Quantity Discount Offer!

- ▶ 20-99 books $13.00 per copy
- ▶ 100-499 books $10.00 each
- ▶ 500-999 books $7.00 each

www.zohrasarwari.com

www.ingramcontent.com/pod-product-compliance
Lightning Source LLC
Chambersburg PA
CBHW020018050426
42450CB00005B/539